FEISTY FIDO
Help For The Leash
Aggressive Dog

Patricia B. McConnell, Ph.D.
Karen B. London, Ph.D.

Cover photo by Gary Baker
Cover Design by Jill Sowe
Typeset by Aimee Moore
Cover Dogs Owned by Ann Gavett
"Mica" (Cattle Dog) and "Ashley" (Labrador Retriever)

For information, contact:
Dog's Best Friend, Ltd.
P.O. Box 447
Black Earth, WI 53515
(608) 767-2435

www.dogsbestfriendtraining.com

Printed in the United States of America

2 3 4 5 6 7 8 9

ACKNOWLEDGEMENTS

Pia Silvani, Director of Pet Training and Behavior at St. Hubert's Animal Welfare Center in Madison, New Jersey came up with the charming name of "Feisty Fido" for dogs who are aggressive to other dogs on leash. We loved the name and we appreciate her graciously allowing us to use it too.

We also want to thank the reviewers of earlier manuscripts: Rebecca Addington, Jacqueline Boland, Lisa Chipongian, Aimee Moore, Pia Silvani, Denise Swedlund, and Chelse Wieland.

We'd like to acknowledge the late John Fisher, John Rogerson, Pia Silvani and Trish King for their creative, practical and humane techniques for helping leash aggressive dogs.

TABLE OF CONTENTS

INTRODUCTION

Every neighborhood has at least one "Feisty Fido," and he can cause a lot of chaos as he barks and lunges at every dog in sight. It's bad enough to have someone else's dog terrorizing the neighborhood, but it's harder still when your own dog is the trouble maker. Just because you want your dog to be polite doesn't mean you know how to make it happen, so many people with reactive dogs find themselves avoiding walks altogether. It becomes a vicious circle—with a lack of both exercise and stimulation leading to a dog who is harder to handle when he is taken on walks. So of course, the walks continue to decrease, and the problems increase. Oh dear...this might be one of the times that a dog owner is wondering why she ever got a dog in the first place.

If you have a dog who fits this description, take heart. There's a lot of good news for owners whose dogs misbehave when walking by other dogs. First of all, if your dog is barking and lunging at other dogs when he's on leash, know that you're not alone. This is a very common behavioral problem, even in dogs who "play well with others" when running free at the dog park.

Although it can initially cause no end of trouble, on-leash dog-dog aggression is one of our favorite behavioral problems, because it has such a high rate of successful treatment. (We use the phrase "on-leash dog-dog aggression" broadly, as it is used by the general public, to mean dogs on leash who growl, lunge, or bark menacingly toward approaching dogs.) Almost all dogs who bark and lunge at passing dogs can be taught "street manners," turning what used to be stressful walks into relaxing strolls.

Be clear, though, that this little booklet isn't designed to create dogs who are good with all other dogs in all situations. If your dog is dog-dog aggressive off leash, the ideas in this booklet won't turn him into the dog everyone loves a doggy day care. What you can get from this booklet is the ability to leash-walk your dog around others, whether it's down the sidewalk or at the vet clinic, knowing that your dog will walk politely by another dog, rather than causing a scene.

Why is My Dog so Rude?

We can't say definitively why so many leashed dogs become rude and reactive when walking by other dogs, but we can make some educated guesses. Some dogs probably feel trapped when they're on leash and are approached by another dog. There's nothing like feeling vulnerable if you're nervous in the first place, and dogs on leashes know they aren't free to run away. Dogs who explode at other dogs for this reason are behaving as though their best defense is a good offense—using the time-honored "I'll get you before you get me" strategy.

There are many reasons why dogs might be nervous about other dogs approaching. Some of them may have been traumatized by another dog and are now afraid of approaching dogs. Perhaps your dog never had a chance to be properly socialized around unfamiliar dogs, and is only comfortable with familiar dogs. Some dogs may be naturally shy around any unfamiliar dog, even though their owners have provided them opportunities to socialize. Genetics plays an important role in all aspects of canine behavior, and shyness is highly heritable, causing even some well-socialized dogs to be nervous around unfamiliar dogs. Whether driven by early experience or genetics (or most likely, both) it's important to understand that dogs who are leery of approaching dogs can respond by barking and lunging toward a dog that frightens them. Just because a dog looks scary to others doesn't mean he's not scared himself. (The big-eyed dog on the cover is a perfect example of that.)

Not all reactive dogs are afraid of other dogs. Some dogs get so excited when they see another dog that they work themselves into a frenzy. If they can't interact, their

2

arousal levels spiral up until they're not only out of their owner's control, they're out of their own control. A high level of emotional arousal, combined with frustration, is a common factor that motivates some dogs to bark and lunge at others. A dog may start out by charging forward to try to play with another dog, but when the leash stops him, over and over, he may learn to associate feeling frustrated with the approach of another dog. As we know from our own species, frustration can fuel aggression like gasoline fuels a fire; "road rage" is a perfect example. Dogs may begin by trying to run over to play with a buddy, but after months and years of being restricted, their energy and frustration can spiral into a cauldron of out-of-control emotions. A dog's tendency to get highly aroused, including a lack of frustration tolerance, can turn an owner's nightly stroll into an unwelcome drama. Sadly, some of the dogs with these tendencies can become truly aggressive, and will eventually take their frustration out on some poor, hapless dog who gets too close.

Another explanation for dogs who bark and lunge at others is a learned association between seeing another dog and the aversive feeling of getting choked by the collar. It's easy to imagine a dog thinking, in some canine kind of way, "I always get hurt when I see another dog on leash, so I'd better not see any dogs today. Uh oh, here comes one now! HEY YOU! You stay away from me—bark bark #@!%#growl. If you get closer I'll get hurt!" Sadly, some owners have been told to give stern leash corrections every time their dog moves toward or growls at another dog. That, of course, confirms the dog's suspicions about the danger of other dogs, and makes him worse. Besides, his dramatic display often does make the other dog go away, so even though he may get a correction from the leash, he still got what he really wanted.

On the other hand, some dogs are just plain bullies, and seem to enjoy the effect of their outbursts. These types of dogs can be taught a more polite response, but are more difficult to teach to be polite in an off-leash environment.

3

Dogs with little experience with other dogs can also have a hard time learning to "play well with others." Polite off-leash play is a big topic that deserves its own book, and is beyond the scope of this booklet. But if you do have a dog who is rude off leash who also barks and lunges on a leash, by all means get the on-leash behavior turned around before you move on to the next step.

So What's an Owner to Do?

In one sense, the solution is simple. Barking and lunging is just one possible reaction to the presence of another dog, and almost any dog can be taught a different reaction. Many dogs who bark and lunge don't behave as though they're aware of an alternative behavior. It's as though they only have one software program installed. But when you teach them a different response, many dogs are happy to use it, and some of them seem downright relieved. For example, if you teach your dog to react to the sight of another dog by looking at you, instead of lunging toward the dog, your problem is basically solved. Sounds simple, and in one sense, it is. But don't stop reading yet. "Simple" isn't the same thing as "easy." After all, how complicated is the concept of getting a golf ball to go into a hole in the ground? It's simple to describe, but a lot of experience is required to get it to work every time, in varying conditions. Teaching your dog to look at you whenever he sees another dog needs to be practiced, just like any sport, until your response and your dog's response become automatic.

This little booklet covers two different behaviors for your dog to learn and eventually perform like a star when he sees another dog. You'll learn when and where to use each of these, so that you're always sure what to do when you encounter another dog. The booklet also has advice for owners of dogs who are so afraid of other dogs that they won't even look at them, what to do when you and your dog are surprised by a loose dog, and how to manage excursions to prevent those oh-so-embarrassing scenes on the sidewalk.

4

The ideas presented here were developed through years of working with clients and their overly reactive dogs. All those years and all those clients have taught us that dogs do better if they and their humans work on perfecting a few, basic exercises rather than learning a multitude of signals that only work part of the time. At face value, the exercises seem almost too simple to be truly useful, sort of a "take two aspirin and call me in the morning" approach to dog training. But again, simple is not easy, and the tricky part is practicing the exercises under gradually increasing levels of distraction. You can help your dog most if you're always aware of what level of distraction you're asking your dog to work within, and if you have realistic expectations of how much to expect of your dog in different contexts. If you and your dog work step-by-step through increasing levels of distraction, eventually both of you will be able to handle the kind of surprise encounters that used to ruin your evening.

The Good Life

Here's what life can look like if you and your dog follow through with the plan:

When he sees another dog approaching, your dog will automatically look away from the dog and look up to your face, without you having to say anything. We call that an "Autowatch," and it's amazing how many dogs can learn to do it—even dogs who, before treatment, looked like maniacs when they saw another dog a block away. Eventually, most dogs will be able to walk right by another dog while politely attending to you.

Additionally, if a dog pops up when you least expect it, you and your dog will effortlessly turn away and stride off in the other direction. (We call that the "U-Turn.") Say, for example, that you're surprised by a dog who just turned the corner in front of you, and is just a few feet away. No barking and lunging from your well-behaved dog, who willingly wheels away from trouble at your side, helping to avoid a confrontation, rather than participating in one.

You and your dog will have an emergency plan for when off-leash dogs come running up to yours (the "Emergency Sit/Stay".) Your dog will go on a reliable Emergency Sit/Stay behind you, while you use new skills to handle the dog charging toward you. Your dog will have more emotional stability, and in any situation, can keep her arousal levels from spiraling up and out of control.

Be Prepared

Start by getting the right equipment, asking yourself if your leash and collar system is helping you, or if it's working against you. Be sure that you're using a leash that gives you the precision you need when you're training your dog—we'd advise a nylon or leather leash that is 6 feet in length. Avoid retractable leashes of any kind, because although they are great on casual strolls, they don't give you the control you need to keep a reactive dog out of trouble.

Collars are even more important when working with a reactive dog, so be thoughtful about what kind of collar you are using. Punitive collars like prong collars and choke collars that tighten as the dog pulls can make the problem worse, and we avoid them like the plague. A much better alternative that works for most dogs is a halter (sometimes called a head collar) such as a Gentle Leader® or a Snoot Loop®. Halters for dogs look like and work like the halter on a horse, and because they control your dog's head, they give you a lot of humane control over your dog's behavior. Halters not only put physics on your side, they avoid triggering a problematic response in dogs who have a learned association between the approach of an unfamiliar dog and a collar tightening around their neck. Halters are safer as well, because pressure around the neck from regular collars can cause serious damage to your dog's throat and spinal column.

If you do change to a halter, get it from someone who is familiar with its use, because the fit of a halter is very important. Most dogs adapt well to them, although all dogs need to get used to these new-fangled things on their faces before they go out into the neighborhood. A small percentage of dogs won't tolerate halters, others have neck or spinal column injuries that preclude the use of halters. These dogs often do well with a harness called the Sensation Harness™. These harnesses are designed so that the leash attaches at the center of your dog's chest, and preclude the pulling problem that regular harnesses create. Some dogs tolerate them better than they do head collars, and become accustomed to them very quickly. If you have a small dog, a regular harness that attaches to the top of your dog's back can work well. But if your dog is over fifteen or twenty pounds, a regular harness just allows your dog to pull you like a wagon, so only use them for small dogs. Limited slip collars (martingales) can be useful for dogs who won't tolerate halters but are too large for harnesses. They only tighten until they're snug around a dog's neck so they're less likely to cause injuries, and can be adjusted so that dogs can't slip out of them. The drawback is that they can still trigger a learned response to a tightening collar, so try another alternative first.

Some highly reactive dogs do best in the initial stages of conditioning to a halter if the owner has both a regular, buckle collar and a halter on the dog, each collar with its own leash. This system provides more security (we've had healthy-looking leashes break, so with some dogs you might want a back up) but it also means more for owners to juggle, so it has both advantages and disadvantages. If you have a dog who tries to slip out of his collar, you can use a martingale and a halter together, hooking the leash to both for safety's sake.

If a dog has caused injury to another dog or has redirected and bitten his owner, a muzzle might be a good idea in the later stages of training. Be sure to introduce the muzzle with lots of treats and very brief sessions (seconds only at first) so that your dog learns to tolerate or even enjoy wearing it. It must fit well; your dog should be comfortable wearing it and able to breathe freely. For extra security, attach the strap through your dog's regular flat collar so it cannot be pawed off. Use caution—never let a muzzled dog overheat. Dogs need to open their mouths to disperse heat, so don't use muzzles on hot days, during exercise or with short-nosed dogs who have trouble breathing normally. We never use muzzles in the early stages of work; they're not necessary when the dogs are far apart. But they can be helpful, both for the dogs and for the comfort of their owners, once the dogs are in close proximity.

Treats—Don't Leave Home Without Them!

Great treats or play toys are essential to success. You're going to be vying for your dog's attention against some pretty impressive competition, so don't go outside armed with a few pieces of kibble or some dry biscuits. You want your dog to really, really want what you've got, so be thoughtful about what kind of food you choose for training. A common mistake is to try a low or medium quality treat, and then conclude that the dog doesn't care about food. Remember that your dog may go crazy for a medium quality treat in the living room, but ignore the same food in the front yard, so pick a food that you know will get your dog's attention no matter what. After all, food is a pretty big category. Isn't your response to stale white bread different than your response to warm, fresh cinnamon rolls? Your dog has preferences too, so experiment and figure out his equivalent of gourmet food and use that for the exercises that follow. Remember that your dog has the final say on what counts as a great treat. If he loves chicken but turns his nose up at liver, don't keep trying liver just because "all dogs like liver!" He might not have read the chapter that says "all dogs like liver," but he'll be happy to tell you what he does love, no matter what the books say. Your dog will love these experiments, and will thank you from the bottom of his heart for buying this booklet.

When you use treats, be sure that they are in a readily accessible place, so that you have them instantly when you need them. Try a bag that attaches around your waist or to your belt and can be opened and closed quickly—in other words, no zipper. Our favorite bait bags are called Quick Draw Training Pouches® (from Legacy by Mail), because you can open and close them easily with one hand.

Be sure your treats are healthy for your dog, and that you're not compromising your dog's weight. Great choices for treats are cooked chicken or turkey, cooked red meat, cooked liver, lightly cooked vegetables like string beans, carrots and peas (our dogs LOVE 'em!) There are lots of good commercial dog treats on the market, but be sure that you are using something that is easily broken into small pieces. You might need to give your dog twenty-five treats in just a few minutes in one session, so you don't want to use pieces that are too big. If your dog is on the hefty side, and you're doing a lot of training, then decrease his meals a bit to compensate. Try to avoid training when your dog is satiated. A little bit of hunger can go a long way.

Food treats aren't the best choice for all dogs. Some dogs will do anything to get to chase their ball, or play tug, or mouth their squeaky toy. If you have a ball-obsessive dog, you probably already know it, but it never hurts to do an experiment. Hold a piece of cooked chicken in one hand and the tennis ball in another. Your dog will tell you which one he wants most. Most dogs choose food (if it's good enough) but if your dog is toy-crazed, then by all means use toys. If you've got that kind of dog, you might save his favorite toy just for training sessions so that it is even more special.

Once the behavior you're working on is well established, you'd be wise to vary the type of reinforcement you give to your dog. We like to alternate between treats, praise and play so that the dog learns to "feel good" when he does what you ask, rather than expecting the same thing every time. In the initial phases, use whatever your dog is most willing to work for, but as you progress, substitute praise or other reinforcements in some of the easier situations. Keep in mind that verbal praise can be a wonderful reward for your dog, but it's rarely enough of a motivation in the initial stages of training, even if you have a voice like Pavarotti. After all, you talk to your dog all day, but how often does he get chicken? For the sake of brevity, we'll use the word "treat" for whatever reinforcement works best for your dog, whether it be food or playing with a favorite toy.

Now that you know what your dog is willing to work for, you're ready to start on the first exercise, which is to teach your dog to turn and look at you whenever he sees an approaching dog.

"WATCH"
A LITTLE EXERCISE WITH BIG RESULTS

Cindy and I didn't have time to look at one another, but if we had, it would've been in horror. Cindy's Weimaraner, Astro, was standing politely on leash beside us, but the two out-of-control Golden Retrievers who were galloping directly at us were harbingers of doom. Astro and Cindy came to me with a serious dog-dog aggression problem, and in the past, this scenario would have ended with a lot of teeth and a lot of trouble. But in a micro-second, Cindy said "Astro, Watch!" and as the Goldens got within inches of her big, gray dog, he did. He turned his muzzle toward her face and kept eye contact with her while I successfully blocked one dog and watched the other bounce off his hindquarters. Astro barely flicked an ear. He continued to look at Cindy while I rounded up the Goldens and herded them away. "Okay," Cindy said. Astro took his eyes off Cindy's face and calmly turned to look at the retreating Goldens. Cindy and I looked at one another in elated surprise, whooped with joy, and fed Astro enough treats to provision a small city.

Patricia McConnell

Right now your dog barks and lunges when she sees other dogs, just like Astro used to do, but what if she had a different response? What if, when she saw another dog, she immediately turned her head and looked at you, wagging her tail in happy anticipation? We call this exercise "Watch"and for a seemingly simple exercise, it has a long list of advantages. First of all, your dog can't bark and lunge toward another dog when her attention is directed to your face. Teaching an incompatible behavior is a time-honored and elegant solution to a lot of behavioral problems, and it works wonderfully with fidos who are a bit too feisty on leash walks. Additionally, by teaching your dog to look at your face when she sees another dog, you're teaching her what you want her to do, rather than hoping she'll figure it out himself. Teaching what's right is almost always more effective than correcting what's wrong. "Just say No" may be a common slogan, but it's not very helpful if your dog has no other response in her repertoire.

One of the reasons that Watch is so effective is that when your dog turns her head and looks at you, she's no longer being stimulated by the sight of the other dog. Rather than seeing an approaching dog and getting revved up, she responds by turning her head away, settling down, and happily anticipating something wonderful (provided by you, of course!) Not only does your dog move backward rather than forward, her emotional response changes from high arousal to relaxed anticipation. She can do it while she's sitting, standing, walking or lying down. It's easy to do and easy to teach—no wonder it works so well. That's the most important reason we recommend teaching dogs to Watch when they see another dog—it works. Over the years, we've found it's the most effective method of all that we've tried, and who are we to argue with success?

We define "Watch" as a cue that directs your dog to look at your face until you release her. But having a dog who'll do a Watch on cue is not the final goal with a dog who's dog-dog aggressive on leash. The goal is having a dog who automatically looks at you as soon as she sees another dog. The approaching dog becomes the stimulus, and now you have a dog who, on her own, responds in a polite and appropriate manner to unfamiliar dogs.

All of this might be hard to imagine if you're working with a dog who charges at other dogs like some pumped-up Green Bay Packer, but take heart. We've seen some dogs who initially became hysterical at the sight of a distant dog, but who ended up being the neighborhood's model dog. One of our clients had that exact experience. Melissa had a large dog named Riley whose behavior toward other dogs made their walks a nightmare. After a few months of working on Watch, she passed a newcomer to the neighborhood, who was walking his two exuberant Irish Setters on the opposite side of the street. She asked her feisty-fido-in-training for a Watch, and without a blink, Riley turned his face to hers. Through her repeated (and relieved) expressions of "good boy, good boy," Melissa heard the man say, "What a sweet dog you have." She learned later that he was concerned about taking his own dogs out now—he feared an unfavorable comparison between his untrained dogs and the real, live Lassie down the block.

In order for Riley to be the neighborhood Lassie, both Melissa and Riley needed to know Watch so well that they could do it even when surprised. Even the simplest exercise can be difficult if you're caught off guard, and that's true for both people and dogs. It's one thing to do simple math in your head at home, but another to add numbers up when you're flustered. And it's one thing for your dog to come when he hears you making supper, and another for him to come when he's playing with others at the park. And so, to insure that Watch works when you need it, you and your dog need to master it in a variety of circumstances. The pros do this as a matter of course, "proofing" a behavior in gradually more distracting environments, never expecting a dog to perform in an environment that is over the dog's head.

Perhaps one of the reasons that many owners don't take the trouble to help their dogs master an exercise is the belief that their dog "knows" how to do it right. But what does "know" mean, anyway? Many dogs "know" how to sit when asked in a quiet place, but don't do it in the confusion of a busy pet store. That's because "knowing" how to do something at home isn't the same as being able to perform it in the middle of distractions. After all, professional tennis players "know" how to hit a perfect serve, but they practice for hours every day to be able to do it under pressure. Give yourself and your dog the same opportunities to master Watch, and it'll pay off in the end.

The simplicity of Watch is especially helpful here—you and your dog can get the basics down fast, so you can spend your time working through increasing levels of difficulty. Once you've got it down when it's calm and quiet, you can start practicing in situations with low-level distractions, then more exciting ones, until you and your dog can whip out a Watch in the midst of chaos without missing a beat.

Getting Started

Start teaching Watch in a quiet place where you're the only show in town, and there's nothing else competing for your dog's attention. Don't underestimate how distracting one of your other dogs can be. Start training when you and your feisty fido are by yourselves. Say "Watch" and wave a moist, smelly piece of food an inch away from your dog's nose. Bring the hand with the food up to your face to lure your dog's eyes up to yours. You can encourage this behavior by smooching or clicking your tongue or moving away a step or two. Once your hand is up by your face, encourage eye contact between you and your dog by smiling, cocking your head, wiggling your finger beside your eye (movement is a great way to keep your dog's attention), and praising with "Good dog. Good dog." Use a voice that is both calm and happy so that your dog knows you're pleased, but that doesn't over stimulate her.

After a second or two (no longer), say "Okay" to release your dog, then give your dog the treat. Be sure you don't move the treat away from your face before you have told your dog, "Okay." If you do, your dog will think the movement is the release, and that could cause you trouble down the road.

Don't worry if your dog appears to be watching the treat and not your face in the early stages of training. Your dog probably is focusing on the treat, but that's fine at this point; you can phase out the treat gradually. If your dog is uncomfortable making eye contact, ask her to focus on your chin. For most dogs, we tend to hold the food at the side of our face by our cheekbone. No matter where your hand ends up, be consistent with the way you move the treat from your dog's nose up to your face, because this movement will become an important visual signal for your dog. Since most dogs learn visual signals before they learn verbal cues, you might confuse your dog if your hand movement is not consistent early on in training.

After you say "Okay," either hand your dog her treat, or toss it on the ground for her. If the dog you're working with doesn't distinguish between treats and fingers, you might want to toss the treat on the ground as soon as you give the release. However, some dogs get so excited about shopping for hidden treats in the grass that you can't get their attention back on you, so use whatever method works best for your dog. Whether you hand feed the treat or toss it, don't try to reinforce the dog while she's in the middle of a Watch. That method works beautifully when teaching a solid Stay, but with Watch it just takes the dog's attention off your face, so say "Gooood" while she's watching you to keep her happy, but deliver the goodies after you release her.

Some dogs have a hard time staying still and focusing on your face when they've seen another dog, and even the best treat in the world is barely enough for them. These dogs do best if the reinforcement for turning their head toward yours is a quick run in the other direction. We were working with a dog just last week whose owner had "tried everything." Her dog leapt and whined and couldn't care less about liver as soon as she saw another dog. But everything changed once a chase game was incorporated into the picture. Now her dog jerks her head toward her owner and they dash off together joyfully. Once they've run about twenty feet, she's thrilled to get an extra bonus of liver. After just a week of work, their progress has been phenomenal, and both of them look equally pleased with themselves—as well they should.

15

Besides knowing what reinforcement works best for your own dog, it's important not to spend too much time teaching your dog to perform long Watches. The valuable part of Watch, and the hardest part for reactive dogs, is to take their attention off that Newfoundland across the street and turn it back to you. Think of how often someone calls your name and you say "Just a minute," while keeping your eyes focused on what you were doing. It's tough for humans to take our attention off something interesting, and it is for your dog too, so reinforce the head turn itself and worry less about the duration of the Watch. Keep Watches especially short in the early stages or training, or when you've asked for a Watch under difficult circumstances.

Oops! My Dog Looked Away Before I Said Okay

Be prepared for your dog to look away before you say "Okay." At first, try to prevent it by asking for a Watch that only lasts a second or two. But as you progress, it's inevitable that your dog's attention will wander, and you need to be mentally prepared. Stay focused yourself, and the microsecond that you see your dog's head starting to turn, quickly move the treat in your hand all the way to your dog's nose. Use that tasty, smelly treat to its greatest advantage by moving it to within a half inch of her nose, and then luring her attention back to you by moving the treat up to your face. If she's looked away, you've probably got some heavy competition for her attention, so get out the big guns and use liver or chicken, or whatever she can't resist. Give her a generous helping of verbal praise the instant she starts to turn her head toward you, even if you had to use food to get it started. Who cares why she's doing it? She's doing it, and that's what matters, and your voice can be used to reinforce her at the exact instant that she starts to look. You might also make smooching noises to redirect your dog's attention. If your dog is too distracted to turn her head after all that, move several feet away from the distraction and try again.

Avoid using the word "Watch" again, even though it's tempting. If you repeat Watch, you're starting over on a brand new Watch, and your dog won't learn that Watch only ends when you say it does. Guard against using it as a punishment ("WATCH#%★&!"). If your dog responds well to "ah ah" or "wrong" or some other quiet sound that means she goofed, go ahead and use it to help her understand that she wasn't supposed to look away. Say it just as your dog starts to look away, but don't say it unless you do it quietly and calmly, otherwise you'll just add to the tension.

Working Up to Real Life

Once you and your dog have mastered Watch in a quiet place with little going on, start asking for Watches when there are mild distractions. Unfamiliar dogs aren't small distractions, they're big ones, so avoid them for now as much as you can. (You might need to avoid neighborhood walks for a few weeks and increase your dog's exercise in the house and yard, if you have one.) A typical progression might include a few days of Watch practice in an empty room or a quiet backyard. The next one or two weeks might be spent asking for a Watch with low to moderate level distractions, perhaps when Ginger is in the front yard and sees a squirrel a block away (not ten feet away!) or turns her head toward an interesting noise.

As soon as Watch is going well at moderate levels of distractions, start asking for it when your dog sees another dog. Of course, you're going to structure this exercise carefully to guarantee that the dog is far away and won't get too much closer. You want your dog to win, so only ask for a Watch if another dog is far enough away that your dog will see him, but not go ballistic. (Later we'll discuss what to do when life happens and you end up with another dog in your face in spite of your best laid plans.)

It's important to structure these sessions so that your dog encounters other dogs at a distance that won't overwhelm her. It helps to brainstorm about situations in which you can predict that you and your dog can see other dogs, but you have complete control over the distance between them. Our clients have worked beside the parking lots of our training centers, vet clinics and pet stores (where you can predict where the other dogs will be and that they'll be on leash), with friends who walk their leashed dogs down certain streets at pre-arranged times, and with dogs in the neighborhood who are always behind fences. Try to anticipate the moment your dog is about to turn her head toward the other dog, and say "Watch" the microsecond she's actually looking toward the dog. Your goal at this stage of training is to set up situations where your dog sees another dog at a distance far enough away that she can still concentrate, to say Watch immediately each time she looks at the other dog, and make her oh-so-glad that she did. This exercise of asking your dog to Watch every time she looks toward another dog is the key to changing your dog's behavior, so plan to spend weeks or months on it. You're working toward a dog who auto-matically looks at you as soon as she spots another dog, so think of it as a sport that requires lots of practice on the fundamentals.

Don't' worry if she looks right back at the other dog as soon as you release her. That's great—she's just given you another opportunity to teach Watch. Most sessions should include a series of Watches in rapid-fire succession, rather than one long Watch that only gives your dog one chance to turn her head and get reinforced for it. You might also want to use Watch in other contexts that don't include dogs. If you use Watch exclusively when you encounter other dogs, Watch will soon mean "Yo! There's another dog somewhere out there." That's actually ideal for some people and their dog, but others might want to keep the signal generalized.

Jackpotting an "Autowatch"

Soon, with practice, your dog will learn that it's fun to look at you when she sees another dog. In fact, rather than feeling tense or frustrated when she spots another canine, she'll start to view it as an opportunity to earn food or a chase game by looking at you. Once she learns the pattern (see dog, look at owner, feel good), eventually she'll anticipate your "Watch" and look at you before you have a chance to say anything. Bingo! That behavior is exactly what you've been working toward. We call it an "Autowatch," meaning that she automatically looked at you when she saw another dog. The first Autowatch is a truly stupendous step. It means that the other dog, rather than your voice, is becoming the cue to look at you. And that's exactly what you want: a dog who automatically looks at you when she sees another dog, rather than automatically barking and lunging toward it.

When you raise a child, your goal is to have her say "please" and "thank you" without having to prompt her. That's the same goal you have for your dog, so be looking for this important change in your dog's behavior, and pull out all the stops when it happens. You know how your dog acts like it's the event of her day when you come home from work? An Autowatch is the event of your day (or week!) and you need to let your dog know it. Rather than running in circles, leaping in the air or rolling over on your back, (well, go ahead if it amuses your dog!) you'll want to give your dog so many treats that she's astounded. Jackpots are just what they sound like—a stupendously better-than-usual reinforcement that amazes your dog and motivates her to look for a chance to do another Autowatch. Once you've gotten the first Autowatch, you might consciously pause before cueing your dog to give her a chance to Autowatch again.

We typically Jackpot by giving a dog 10 to 15 pieces of an extra yummy treat one at a time, in rapid succession, while gushing that she is the most wonderful dog in the entire world. You can say "Good dog" over and over and over—at least once for each of those 10 to 15 treats; you can laugh and sing or make any foolish fuss that your dog would enjoy. Do anything that knocks her little socks off, so she'll remember it and work for it to happen again.

Guard against doing something that you love but your dog might not, like petting her when she really wants more treats, or hugging her in that rude way we primates have of expressing affection. If you make Autowatches the highlight of her day, she'll start looking for dogs on her own, so that she can whip her head toward you and get a goody. And there you are—now you have a dog who reacts to the sight of other dogs by looking at you, rather than barking and lunging away from you. That calls for a deep breath, a big smile, and a Jackpot of your own!

In addition to Jackpotting for Autowatches, you can give your dog a Jackpot if she responds properly when asked to perform a difficult Watch. Say a dog surprises you both and appears much closer than the distance at which you've been practicing. You blurt out Watch without thinking, and are simply amazed that it worked. Oh wow! That was hard, but your dog pulled it off, so let her know that she just won the canine equivalent of a trip to Hawaii.

Insuring a Thoughtful Training Progression

The least intuitive part of training a new behavior is one of the most important, and that's asking your dog to perform in circumstances that are gradually more and more difficult. A common training mistake is, for a week or so, asking for Watches when it's relatively easy for your dog, then skipping over moderate levels of difficulty, and proceeding directly to asking when it's truly difficult. The dog can't handle that level of difficulty and fails miserably. An analogy is going from regular ice skating to doing a triple lutz at the Olympics. After a few sessions of being over their heads, both dogs and humans can get pretty discouraged. But a little

20

thoughtful planning can avoid that problem, and lead to a gold medal performance in the long run.

Take the time to write out a list of circumstances in which is it Easy, Moderate, Difficult and Really Hard for your dog to perform a Watch. Every dog is different of course, but here's a sample list to provide direction, for a dog we'll call Muffin, who is being asked to Watch in the following situations.

Easy
- In the kitchen before dinner, no one else home (easiest).

- In the backyard on a quiet morning, no one in sight (a little harder than the kitchen, because the great outside always has at least interesting smells around, but still relatively easy.)

Moderate
- In the backyard, when Muffin sees a squirrel three houses away.

- In the kitchen, when the kids are home from school.

- In the front yard, with people (who Muffin loves) walking across the street.

- In the parking lot of the training center, where Muffin is 50 yards away from the path of another dog.

- On the sidewalk, as Muffin walks toward a dog she is friendly with, who is 25 yards away.

- On the sidewalk, as Muffin sees a dog who she's charged at numerous times in the past, who is about a block away.

Difficult
- In the backyard, when Muffin flushes a squirrel just ten feet away that dashes up the tree.
- On the sidewalk, when Muffin wants to greet her doggy buddy who is just 3 feet away and play bowing.

- On the sidewalk, when Muffin looks at an unfamiliar dog who is 30 feet away, and walking toward you both.

- On the sidewalk, when Muffin sees a dog who's a third of a block away that she's charged at before.

Really Hard!
- On the sidewalk, when an unfamiliar dog walks by.

- At the vet clinic, 10 feet away from two other dogs, who are barking.

- At the training center, 2-3 feet off line from the path of dogs going to the training room.

- On a walk when two off-leash dogs run up to your dog and try sniffing her while their owner grins from a block away saying "It's Okay! My dogs LOVE other dogs!!"

Of course every dog is different. Some dogs will be relatively relaxed with other dogs at 15 feet, and only react if the dog comes within 3 feet of her. Others bark and charge toward other dogs who are a block away. Only you know your dog well enough to structure a customized plan that helps your dog through each level of difficulty so that she can master each one as she goes. Keep in mind that the "Easy" level of difficulty requires the least time and energy. It's the "Moderate," "Difficult" and "Really Hard" ones that need to be mastered. Always be on the lookout for subtle signs that your dog is becoming overwhelmed, whether it's tongue flicking, freezing, looking away, refusing a favorite treat, or obsessively sniffing the ground, and do everything you can to end on a good note.

22

When Not to Use "Watch"

As you and your dog work on Watch, methodically setting up situations that your dog can handle, you will still be running into that thing called "Life." There will be neighbors walking their dogs when you least expect it, a doggy birthday party down the block, a man with his two dogs running up to you to ask directions, or any of a number of other Feisty Fido debacles just waiting to happen. If you know in your heart of hearts that pigs will fly before your dog will do a Watch, don't even bother to ask. There's no profit in setting your dog up to fail. If a situation is more than you and your dog can handle gracefully, move without pause to your backup plans. Plan B involves getting out of the situation with a U-Turn or with an Emergency Sit/Stay (details in the next sections.) Whatever you do, don't ask for a "Watch" knowing that only a miracle is going to make it happen. It's great to believe in miracles, but wise owners never count on them.

Summary

• Use "Watch" to get your dog's attention the instant she looks at another dog.

• Start by teaching Watch with no other dogs around, and gradually work up to situations that include them. Avoid expecting too much too soon.

• Help your dog at first by using a tasty treat to lure her nose toward your face right after you say quietly say "Watch."

• Once she's looking at your face, say "Gooood dog" and move your finger and/or head while she's watching you.

• Avoid repeating the word "Watch" or saying it in a tension-filled voice.

• Clearly release your dog ("Okay" or "Free") and reinforce with treats, toys or a chase game.

• If your dog looks away, bring the treat back to her nose and lure her gaze up again without repeating "Watch."

• Keep the duration of Watch very brief, especially in early stages of training.

• Jackpot for Autowatches or other exceptional performances.

• Turn and move away if your dog is overwhelmed; then ask for a Watch when she's far enough away from the other dog to calm down.

USING A "U-TURN"
TO LEAVE TROUBLE BEHIND

Bugsy stiffened and leaned forward, the hair along his back went up, and he let out a series of deep, rough barks. These weren't his usual excited barks; they were the low-pitched, menacing ones that put you on alert to trouble. Alarmed, I turned in the direction he was facing to see a coyote, strolling down the road 20 feet away. I was flabbergasted, and if I may indulge myself and speak for him, Bugsy was, too. He began leaping and lunging, and was as distracted as I'd seen him in almost a year.

There was no question that Bugsy's Watch cue wouldn't work in that extraordinary circumstance, so I immediately converted to Plan B, which was getting out of the situation as fast as our legs could carry us. Without taking the time to think about it, we made a U-turn and headed off in the opposite direction, just as we had practiced in case of an emergency. We kept moving in the other direction until the local Wylie E. Coyote was out of sight. If it had been an actual dog we had seen 20 feet away, a Watch would have worked just fine. After months of practice, Bugsy can do Autowatches almost any time he sees a dog, and can even handle an off-leash dog who takes us by surprise. But a coyote? That definitely qualified as an emergency. We don't use "U-Turns" very often, but when we do, it's always with a feeling of relief at having dodged a bullet.

Karen London

As you can see, a "U-Turn" is a great tool to have in your training repertoire. A U-Turn is exactly what it sounds like: you and your dog are walking forward, and on your cue, you both instantly turn 180 degrees and move in the opposite direction. Your dog turns because he knows your cue means: "Quick! We're going to play the turn-around-really-fast-and-go-the-other-way game!" Your dog doesn't turn because he hits the end of the leash. That would increase the tension and could elicit the very behavior you're trying to avoid. He turns because he knows the game, hears the cue and almost without thinking, wheels away from trouble.

Like Watch, the action itself is simple, but it needs to be mastered to be truly useful. And like Watch, a U-Turn is another behavior that is incompatible with your dog barking and lunging at another dog. A U-Turn differs from a Watch cue in that you use it when you know your dog will be too aroused to perform a Watch or if your dog barks and lunges at another dog. The goal of a U-Turn is to get you out of sticky situations, and if you and your dog master both the Watch and the U-Turn, you'll be able to handle most of the situations that life can throw at you.

Say, for example, that you've been working on the Watch cue, and your dog will look at you every time he sees a dog from fifteen to fifty feet away. You've been doing a good job of going step-by-step, so you haven't yet progressed to asking for a Watch when the other dog is only ten feet away. Then all of a sudden one evening, you and your dog round a corner and practically run into a Great Dane. There you both are, half a second away from your dog being an idiot. This is no time to ask for a Watch from your dog—it's time to get the heck out of Dodge. Few of us, dogs or humans, can think fast and clearly when we're shocked and surprised, so your best action here is to turn and move away. If you and your dog practice this exercise so that it's second nature, you'll be able to do it when you don't have time to think, and that, after all, is when you need it.

One of our clients used it when she and her dog were surprised at a vet clinic. Usually, Mary avoided dramatic confrontations in the waiting room by coming in after regular hours. But on one particular evening, entering what she thought would be an empty lobby, Mary and her dog walked smack into the path of another dog. Without thinking, as if on auto-pilot, she said "Turn!" and pivoted around to her right. Just as fast, her dog turned and strode safely with her out into the parking lot. We wish you could have seen Mary's face as she told us about her victory. "It was amazing! A few months ago that situation would have been a disaster, but both of us turned so fast we didn't even realize what we'd done until we'd done it! After it all sunk in, I was exhilarated, and I swear my dog was just as pleased as I was."

You can use this technique any time you need to avoid trouble, whether it be a terrier barking hysterically on the sidewalk, or a surprise encounter with a Chesapeake Bay Retriever. We've learned that some dogs are happy to be helped out of a troublesome situation, and become less reactive in the future. Perhaps these dogs learn to trust that they'll be protected from confrontations rather than forced into situations they can't handle. U-Turns come with an added bonus—they can be handy for those distractions that your dog just can't resist if they're too close, like pesky squirrels or in-line skaters.

The key to deciding when to use a Watch and when to use a U-Turn is knowing what level of distraction your dog can handle. When you're working on Watch, you are gradually raising the intensity of the distraction, conditioning your dog to turn away from events that increase in difficulty. Eventually, you can expect your dog to react calmly to a surprise encounter that happens right beside you. But it's not fair to ask your dog to Watch when he hasn't worked up to that level of distraction. Think of it like a sport— you'd never expect basketball player to make every free throw at the big game if he hadn't practiced at home. Turning away from trouble is much easier for most dogs than staying still and containing all of their emotions, so U-Turns work better than Watches when your dog's abilities are being challenged. Of course, we all want our dogs to be able to walk or stand politely while other dogs walk by, but while you're working on that, U-Turns can keep you out of trouble. If you ask for a quick U-Turn in a situation that is over your dog's level of training, you're doing a lot more than avoiding trouble. You're teaching a response that is incompatible with barking and lunging, and helping your dog be the good citizen we all want him to be.

In a way, a U-Turn teaches your dog to do the same thing as a Watch. Both cues result in a dog who turns away from another dog and moves in the opposite direction. Watches ask for a turn of the head, while a U-Turn involves the whole body. For most dogs, U-Turns are easier because once turned around they can't see the dog anymore and have moved on to other things. Some dogs adore the part where they get to chase after you, and enjoy that reinforcement more than a treat. We've found both cues to be useful for the dogs we've worked with, so think of Watch and U-Turn as complementary cues that you can mix and match depending on your dog and the circumstances.

Getting Started

Before you start training your dog to do a U-Turn, decide what verbal cue you are going to use. Ideally, it should be a sound that you can say quickly and easily. Be sure that it doesn't sound like any of your other signals—for example, if you use "No! " to stop your dog, then using "Go!" for a U-Turn is probably not such a great idea. Some examples that clients have used are "This Way," "Let's Go," (the "go" here probably doesn't get confused with "no" because the cue starts with "let's"), "Wow!," "Oh No!," "Now!," "Turn" and "Oh boy!" Avoid using words you've used before, like "Come" and the dog's name, so you can start out fresh. We're going to use "Turn" in this booklet, because that's what we want you and your dog to do, but we like the sound of "Let's Go" best when working with a dog. Most importantly, pick one that you like and that won't confuse your dog. Don't fuss too much over finding the perfect word, just be consistent once you decide and use the same tone of voice you'd use when surprised yourself.

As with any new behavior, be sure to teach this exercise in a calm, quiet place. Start where you and your treats (or toys) are the only game in town. Quiet backyards or empty long hallways will make it easier for both you and your dog to concentrate. With great treats or your dog's absolute favorite toy in your right hand, stride forward with your dog on your left. (Reverse these directions if you walk with your dog on your right side.) Don't worry about getting him in a perfect heel position, but don't initiate your first U-Turn on cue if he's more than a body length ahead of you. If he gets that far ahead, just turn around and walk forward again. Now you're in front and can start your U-Turn as he gets even with you.

When your dog is beside or a tiny bit in front of you, and you are moving forward briskly, say "Turn" in an excited voice, and pivot around your right leg, turning your body to the right. You'll end up facing 180 degrees from where you were going, continuing to walk forward.

Unless you encourage your dog to turn with you, he'll probably keep going straight the other way, so help him get it right by doing one or all of the following:

1) *Have a great treat or toy* in your right hand, and use it to lure your dog around with you as you turn. Be sure to move the treat within an inch of your dog's nose (that might mean moving your right arm across your body to your left side where your dog's nose is), and then lure the dog around your legs as you turn, like a carrot leading a donkey.

2) *Bend your knees as you turn.* Most dogs respond beautifully when you dip your knees a bit while turning, perhaps because it's a clear visual signal at their eye level, or perhaps because it's what ethologists call an "intention movement" that signals impending action. Whatever the reason, it will make a big difference in your dog's response.

3) *In the early training stages, use sound to get your dog's attention.* After you say "Turn," tongue clicks and smooches are powerful sounds that help get your dog's attention on you, and off of what's in front of him. Be sure to say "Turn" first, or the other sounds will become the cue. Guard against using clicks or smooches too much, but they can be helpful in the early stages to get your dog's attention.

4) *Sometimes it helps to slap your left leg to keep your dog close to you as you pivot,* but be sure not to do that if you're holding the leash in that hand. If you have the leash in your hand while you pat your leg, the leash will slap your dog in the face if he's in the right position—not exactly a positive reinforcement.

For the first two or three sessions, say "Good Dog!" and give your dog a treat the instant that he completes the turn. We have the most luck with verbal praise given in a pleased, but not too exuberant voice. After all, you want your dog to be happy he turned with you, but you also want him to move in a calm and contained manner. Don't stop to do this—you need to keep moving forward, but as you move, slip that great treat you're holding into your dog's mouth. If you're using a toy, throw it straight out in front of you and let your dog run and get it. Timing is everything here, so be sure to reinforce your dog as soon as you can after he's turned and changed direction, even if it's a bit sloppy or slow at first.

What's important in these first sessions is that you and your dog, more or less together, turn 180 degrees, continue moving briskly forward but in the opposite direction, and most importantly, your dog is thrilled about the whole thing. Once the two of you are getting adept at pivoting around together, delay the reinforcement until you've taken a few strides forward after the turn.

Getting It to Work When You Need It

Once your dog will "Turn" with you in the quiet of your backyard, it's time to start asking him to do it when he's distracted. Eventually, of course, you'll use it for the Big Kahuna of distractions—a dog who pops up like a piece of toast right in front of you, but you need to work your way up to that gradually. As we mentioned earlier in the Watch section, this is the part of training that most people mess up (speaking scientifically, of course.) It seems to be very common for dog owners to expect their dogs to go from Step One ("Turn" when there is no distraction) to Step Twenty-Five ("Turn" when four Golden Retrievers magically appear in front of you) without practicing the steps in between. But the pros know working on the middle steps makes the difference between success or failure, so be sure to construct a plan that gives your dog lots of practice at Step Two to Twenty-Four before expecting him to work at Step Twenty-Five.

Begin the middle steps by asking your dog to "Turn" away from a distraction that is far less stimulating than another dog. Choose anything that your dog will focus on and want to move toward, such an approaching person, a familiar dog that your dog gets along well with (and who isn't too terribly close by), or a ball in the grass that your dog would like to pick up. Your goal is to set up situations in which your dog will see something that not only gets his attention, but that is something he would tend to move toward. As he looks at whatever distraction you've chosen, ask for a Turn. Remember to help him out with your voice and your body as you did when you first started, because in a way, you are starting over. Turning away from *something* is a lot different than turning away from *nothing*, so in one sense, it's a whole new game he's learning.

Because you've upped the difficulty of the exercise, initially reinforce even the slightest turn of his head away from the distraction. As he gets more practice at this level of

31

distraction, you can start to expect more from him before he gets the treat. If he ignores you and keeps looking forward, move your hand with the treat or toy all the way to his nose, and then lure his head around like a carrot and a donkey. Be sure the food gets to within an inch or so of his nose, and use your body (dip your knees, turn your chest to the right) and your voice to help him change his focus. Even if you had to use everything in your repertoire to get him to turn, give him a big, wonderful treat once he's facing the other way. GOOD BOY! If you can, try again with the same distraction until you see even a modest improvement, being sure to make him oh-so-glad that he turned with you.

Of course the speed at which dogs respond varies tremendously, but most dogs need two to eight weeks of practice at moderate levels of distractions before you can expect it to work smoothly in a crunch. Just as you did with the Watch signal, write out a list of examples of Easy, Moderate, Difficult and Really Hard distractions before you start working on them. Your goal, just as it is with Watch, is to gradually increase the difficulty of the exercise, and that means you must have a clear idea of what is easy and what is difficult for your dog.

Every dog is different, but here's an example of what Easy, Moderate, Difficult and Really Hard distractions might look like for a dog named George:

Easy
• George spots two people he knows who are approaching 50 yards away.

• George starts to sniff a moderately interesting spot on the grass.

• He hears a motorcycle and looks toward it, but it's out of sight.

Moderate
- George sees two children whom he just adores, but they are over 50 yards away.

- George sees a dog he's comfortable with, who is 20 yards away.

- An unfamiliar dog is walking toward you and George, but he is 100 yards away.

Difficult
- An unfamiliar dog, only 20 yards away, is walking toward you and George.

- George's two best doggy buddies are playing together just ten feet in front of him.

- George is sniffing, and about to eat a greasy food wrapper on the ground.

Really Hard
- An unfamiliar dog is trotting toward you, only fifteen feet away.

- A dog the size of Connecticut rounds the corner eight feet in front of you and surprises you both.

It's impossible to make a useful generalization about how long you need to practice at each level of distraction. It depends on many aspects of the dog himself, including how serious the problem is, and how often you are able to practice. Some dogs can work through to very difficult levels in four to eight weeks, although it's more realistic to think of treating a feisty fido as a four to six month treatment plan. Dogs who have had little socialization, who have serious problems with arousal, or are highly motivated to bark and lunge, can take longer. Many dogs are never "done" and will always need practice and thoughtful attention to how much they can handle.

U-Turns work best if they are not over used. We'd advise never asking your dog to do difficult ones more than two or three times in a row, and to watch for any signs of stress (tongue flicks, yawns, tense body postures, avoiding you, rejecting a favorite treat or sniffing the ground obsessively.) If you see any of those signs, then go back a step or two and end on a good note. Your training will progress best if you can manage to ask for one to five U-Turns each day, but never with all of them at a challenging level of difficulty. Don't downplay the value of asking for just one good U-Turn, rewarding it with enthusiasm and then moving on to something else. Repetition isn't always a good thing if the exercise is a bit stressful, and we've learned in our Feisty Fido classes that a little bit of this goes a long way.

When "Life" Happens

If and when you have to use your U-Turn in an emergency, be sure to continue striding away from the other dog to a distance at which your dog can control himself. Stop, breathe, collect yourself and help your dog do the same, and then ask for a Watch. You might want to add in some play as a tension reliever when you're well out of trouble. Whew! Disaster averted! The beauty of U-Turns is that they help you avoid trouble not just by turning away from it, but by putting some distance between you and whatever it is that could've overwhelmed your dog. U-Turns help you prevent that bad habit of over reacting, and get you and your dog to a distance where you can go back to asking for a Watch. Think of Watch as your primary equipment and a U-Turn as an accessory, and you'll be ready for just about anything.

Summary

• Use a U-Turn in emergencies to prevent your dog from regressing back to rude behavior.

• To accomplish the turn, say "Turn!" (or "Let's Go!" or whatever cue you choose to use), dip your knees and as you do, pivot around your right leg.

• Use short, repeated notes like smooches or tongue clicks to stimulate your dog to pivot with you, and use a treat or toys to lure him into a turn.

• Stride briskly out of the turn and continue to walk in the opposite direction.

• Give your dog a treat the instant he turns in the first few sessions, and after he's turned and taken several strides in a new direction during later sessions.

• Start with no distractions, and gradually work up to asking him to do a U-Turn in the presence of other dogs.

• If at all possible, once you've used the U-Turn in an emergency, ask your dog to Watch at a distance at which he can control himself.

THE EMERGENCY SIT/STAY AND OTHER USEFUL PANIC BUTTONS

The Emergency Sit/Stay

Everyone with a leash-aggressive dog has the same nightmare: While you're out politely walking Fido on leash, three unleashed Gordon Setters come tearing down the block straight at you. Usually this is accompanied by a hale and hearty wave from the Gordons' owner who yells: "It's Okaa-aay, they LOVE other dogs!" If you had time, you'd yell back "No it's not Okay, my dog is about to EXPLODE!" But you don't have time to respond, because you're too busy having a heart attack.

Given that this situation is almost inevitable, no matter how early in the morning you walk your dog, it's helpful to have a plan that both you and your dog can pull off in emergencies. That's where the Emergency Sit/Stay comes in. It looks like this: when you see a loose dog (let's just start with one!) running toward you, you instantly put your dog on a sit/stay to your side and one step behind you. Confident that your own dog will stay where you placed her, you stride one step forward toward the approaching goof ball, and command him to sit. Amazingly, he probably will. (If this seems unlikely, bear with us—we'll talk a little later about how surprisingly easy it can be to make this happen.) Depending on the dog, you either tell him to stay where he is, or you toss treats behind him, and then you and your dog slide off in the other direction. All this time, you've been between your own dog and the approaching one. You're basically managing two dogs at once, and although it may sound difficult at first, it works surprisingly well in many situations. It's kept us out of trouble no small number of times, so we encourage you to add it to your tool box.

Getting Started

As usual, start in a quiet place with no distractions—just you and your dog. As you and your dog walk forward together, ask her to sit when she is slightly behind you and to one side or another (pick one and stick with it.) The trickiest part for some dogs is to learn to sit when she's not facing you. If you've worked in obedience competition or done a lot of heel work, this will be trivial for your dog. If you haven't, your dog will want to swing around to the front of you, face you and then sit. If this happens, work to prevent it by using food to lure her into the right position, facing the same way as you.

Next, ask your dog to "Stay" and take one step forward while she stays quietly behind you. Step back to where you started and slip your dog a treat while she's holding her stay, all the while quietly praising her for being such a good girl. Release quietly (to keep the arousal level low) and start again. Your goal at this point is to help your dog to be comfortable on a Stay while you move a few steps forward away from her. Once she's rock solid at that, start blurting out "Sit! Stay!" with a bit more tension, as you would if you really were surprised by a galloping greyhound. Gradually add in gestures and vocal commands to non-existent dogs, asking your own dog to stay while you take your attention off her and commence communicating with a phantom dog. Initially you should work without a dog present; just pretend that there's one there so that your dog gets used to your strange behavior without the distraction of a real dog.

Once your dog will stay while you work with imaginary dogs, it's time to practice on some real ones. Enlist the help of your friends, so that you can structure the sessions within the skill level of you and your dog. Of course, initially the other dogs should be on leash and stopped well before they get too close to you; you can work up to closer encounters as you and your dog progress. Obviously, you're still going to try to avoid unfamiliar off-leash dogs in real life, but if you can, set up this "advanced" stage of practice with a familiar dog that your dog likes so that you can both get ready for the real thing.

Handling the Other Dog

You can see that the basics are very simple: teach your dog an Emergency Sit/Stay so that you can get between her and the approaching dog. Then focus your attention on blocking the other dog's access to your own and slide away while the other dog is distracted. This is most successful is you have a variety of tricks up your sleeve. Our first option is to say "Sit!" since so many dogs know it and seem to do it without thinking, no matter who says it. It helps tremendously to add a visual signal—swoop your hand upward in an exaggerated sit signal and you'll radically improve the chances that the approaching dog will comply. In our experience, many dogs in this context don't actually sit, but they stop and stand still, taking their attention off your dog and putting it on you, where you want it.

Other effective actions include throwing a handful of treats behind the approaching dog to get his attention away from your dog. You could even throw the treats straight at the dog's face to distract him even further. Some people have pulled out their trusty umbrellas and opened it abruptly toward the other dog as he runs at them. If you have no other recourse, you can try acting like a soccer goalie, and block the dog's access to yours with a "body block." There's a slightly higher risk level associated with this, in that you're putting your own body in potential harm's way, so don't do this unless you are willing to take a bit of a risk. In our experience, most dogs are focused on your dog and have no interest in causing you harm, but you'll have to make your own decision if you're in that situation. Ideally, you'll have stopped the dog long before that, and you and your dog can slide quietly away while your unwelcome visitor snarfs food up in the grass.

Needless to say, all of these sounds and actions can pull your own dog off of a solid Stay, so your training should include lots of positive reinforcement for holding her position no matter what you're doing. In between your weird shenanigans directed toward the other dog, turn and give your dog a treat while she's on her stay so that even though she might think you're crazy, she's still glad she's staying where she is. Along with treats, we like to include quiet praise for our own dogs ("You are SUCH a good girl for being so polite and quiet, good GOOD girl!") along with the authoritative signal you're giving the other dog.

Most often the Emergency Sit/Stay looks something like this: you quickly but quietly tell your own dog to "Sit and Stay" behind you. You move between your dog and the unfamiliar dog, authoritatively tell the approaching dog to "Sit and Stay" with actions and words. If it works, you throw a handful of treats behind or at the other dog and slide away while he eats them. (Be cautious about using a release word here, or you might confuse your own dog. Most approaching dogs won't hesitate to break a stay to go after the food you threw.) If "Sit and Stay" doesn't work, throw the treats right at the dog's face, and keep throwing until you can distract him enough to move safely away

Most of our clients thought we were crazy when we brought this method up, because they didn't believe it would work. And it won't every time, we'd bet on it. But it works an impressive amount of the time, so it's well worth the practice it will take to add it to your repertoire.

Other Options in an Emergency

An Emergency Sit/Stay is a valuable tool, but it always helps to have some other ideas in your mental toolbox. We offer some here, but you know your dog and your circumstances better than anyone, so do your own brainstorming about other ways to take quick action when necessary. In an emergency, you don't have time to think through a perfect response, so make your decisions ahead of time. Then when the time comes, you're mentally ready to take effective action that turns a potential crisis into a training victory.

Some of our clients have planned out escape routes that they could safely use if need be—a driveway, an alley, behind a car, or down a different street. If there's nowhere to go, you could try putting a handful of treats one inch from your dog's nose to keep his attention off the approaching dog and move as fast as you can in another direction. If an encounter is inevitable, guard against pulling tightly on your dog's leash. That will just add tension and make matters worse. With some dogs, in some situations, it can actually help to drop the leash completely, but because of the obvious safety concerns with that suggestion, we wouldn't advocate it except on an individual case-by-case basis. Often dogs will do better if you jolly them up with a lilting, happy voice, as long as your voice is relaxed. Be sure to avoid stiffening your body and holding your breath. Those are both signs of tension to dogs and can only contribute to their arousal, so consciously breathe deeply and keep your body loose and fluid. Often it helps to turn and move a step or two away from your dog and the "visitor," encouraging them to come with you on a walk rather than all of you focusing on an extended greeting that may lead to trouble.

No matter what your plan is, stay as calm and relaxed as possible. Fake it if you have to (remember to breathe!), because your demeanor can either escalate the tension or calm things down. And remember, even an unfortunate setback doesn't mean you've lost all the great progress you've made so far. If you do have a set back, organize a planned training encounter in a similar context at which you and your dog can succeed. It will help you both put that nasty surprise behind you, where it belongs. Tomorrow is always another day, and thank heaven for that.

TRAINING TIPS WORTH REMEMBERING

While every situation is unique, it's worth reviewing some basics that can make the difference between success and failure in any training program. Professionals in every field stress the importance of paying attention to the fundamentals, so take a tip from them and be sure you've mastered the points that follow.

Be Sure You Have What Your Dog Wants

Remember that your dog gets to say what is a reinforcement and what isn't. Your first job is to find what your dog is willing to work for, so that you can get his attention in the midst of mild or moderate distractions. Don't give up until you've found something that works. (We've stooped to rabbit skins, dead pigeons, used tissues and sheep poop, along with golden oldies like cooked turkey, liver, tennis balls and squeaky toys.) Don't forget to include a good chase game as a great reinforcer for many dogs, especially ones who turn up their noses to leg of lamb.

Start in Easy Situations

Keep your eventual goal of passing right by another dog on the sidewalk in your mind's eye, but remember that the way to get there is to help your dog succeed at each step along the way. Be very thoughtful about practicing in a series of situations that are closer and closer approximations of that final goal. Step by step, slow and steady, onward and upward, Rome wasn't built in a day . . . you get the idea. As simple as it sounds, this is the aspect of training that novices don't seem to get, so concentrate on going one step at a time because even though it makes sense, it doesn't seem to be something that we humans naturally do when training our dogs.

Start with no distractions at all and gradually work up to mild, moderate and then difficult ones. This gradual increase in the intensity of distractions applies within single training sessions and from one training session to the next.

The Right Kind of Repetition is Critical

That doesn't mean that you ask your dog to Watch twenty times in a row every session. What it does mean is that for these ideas to work, you've got to practice them enough that the exercises become second nature to you both. In the early stages of training your dog will learn fastest if each session includes lots of repetition. For example, you might ask your dog to Watch twenty-three times in one ten-minute session with a friend's dog. We have the best luck with asking for a Watch five to seven times in a row, then giving the dog a break (sniff the ground, belly rubs) and beginning again.

Within any series of repetitions, the easiest exercise should come first. We like to do the easiest exercise 1-2 times, then increase the difficulty slightly for 1-2 trials and then, if and only if the dog is doing well, increase it slightly again for a trial or two. However, we don't advise that you always use a simple, linear progression. Sometimes it's useful to end on a few easier versions, and sometimes we think it's best to intersperse a few easier exercises within the progression from easy to hard. If, for example, you ended the last Watch session with an unfamiliar dog 20 feet away, you might ask for a Watch at the following distances, in the following order: 25 feet, 22 feet, 20 feet, 17 feet, 17 feet, 15 feet, 20 feet. Of course, the details depend on the dog, but in all cases the most work should go into the "middle" steps, instead of skipping from "easy" to "really hard" with little work in between.

Once your dog has gotten the hang of it, don't ignore the value of asking for a Watch or U-Turn just once, and then moving on to something else if the dog did well. What's most important is to end on a good performance, and to insure that your dog is really glad he did what you asked, because you made it fun.

Be Flexible

Just because he was brilliant yesterday, doesn't mean he'll be brilliant today. Don't let it throw you. Maybe your dog is agitated because of the weather, or a distant dog barking, or because of something he ate. Perhaps a new puppy down the block got your dog aroused at eleven o'clock, and even though you've forgotten it by the two o'clock session, he hasn't. There are lots of events during the day that can change your dog's overall level of arousal in ways that aren't noticeable, at least not until you challenge him with a Feisty Fido exercise.

If you can't figure out why he's acting differently on a particular day, don't fuss over it too much. Dogs are just like us—they have good days and bad days. You're better off not worrying about why Fido had a bad day, and just rolling with the punches. (The exception is if your dog steadily regresses rather than improves, then it's time to re-evaluate your program.)

Rolling with the punches means you adjust the bar to how your dog is doing that particular day. It takes a lot of flexibility and faith not to get hung up in your expectations and to work with what you've got, so read this section every morning. It helps many people to keep a journal, so that you can keep your eye on the big picture, and not be discouraged by minor glitches in the progression.

Both trainers and laboratory behaviorists know that what looks like a setback is often followed by a particularly great session, so keep the faith, lower your standards if your dog is struggling, and look forward to the next leap of progress.

End on a Good Note

If your dog has had some difficulty with a particular series of exercises, drop the difficulty level way down so that you can end on a good note. If, on the other hand, your dog is doing great and you're pumped up with enthusiasm, be sure to stop before you push the boundaries so far that he inevitably starts to fail. A friend of ours summed up a common, although inadvertent training schedule when she said, "Good grief. I just realized what I've been saying to my dog is 'You're going to do it until you get it wrong!' "

We've also learned by trial and error that the hardest time to stop is often the best time to stop. Stop when you're flush with excitement, even when you want to keep going, before the next exercise goes south on you. It also helps to keep in mind that many dogs show their improvement between sessions and not during them, so don't keep pushing a dog if you feel like you're not getting far enough. Stop on a good note, even if you have to go out of your way to create it, and then evaluate your progress in the next session.

PREVENTION

An Ounce of Prevention . . .

In some ways, your dog's reaction to other dogs is like a bad habit. Every time she barks and lunges, she's like a would-be quitter having just one more cigarette. Keeping this in mind, anything you can do to prevent an incident is worth doing. Prevention is not giving up. It's a way of protecting your dog from situations that may overwhelm or frighten her and act to reinforce those old, bad habits.

You've probably already spent a lot of time trying to prevent incidents while walking in the neighborhood, but it always helps to review what you're doing now to stay out of trouble while you're working on a treatment plan. Most people with feisty fidos try to walk their dogs at quiet times of day. (We've learned to assume any dog out walking at 5:30 AM might be trouble!) When you do encounter another dog, don't hesitate to cross the street or turn and go the other way. To make this possible, try to walk on streets that have little traffic. Obviously, you're already avoiding streets with dogs running loose, but you might also want to look out for yards with high hedges that may conceal approaching dogs until they are too close. Most importantly, if any situation makes you feel concerned, avoid it. Many of our clients skipped their neighborhood walks during the early stages of training, and found other ways to exercise their dogs. Don't think you're being a wimp for avoiding trouble. You're being a wise and thoughtful dog owner with a carefully thought out rehabilitation plan.

Manners Matter at Home Too.

Remember that your dog is always learning, whether you're in "training mode" or not. Because of that, it's important to insure that your dog isn't spending the day unlearning what you're trying to teach during organized

45

training sessions. This happens most often in houses where dogs can bark out the window or from behind the fence at other dogs passing by. If you're teaching your dog a behavior incompatible with barking and lunging, you're not going to get very far if the same dog barks and lunges at other dogs when she's at home. If your dog can bark at other dogs from inside the living room or the back yard, then why wouldn't she bark at them when she's out and about?

For that reason, prevent owner-absent barking by blocking your dog's view of passing dogs. Close the curtains, block the windows with poster board, or move the dog into a crate or back room where she can't see out the window. You wouldn't leave a five-year old home alone with unlimited amounts of candy, so help your dog by taking away the temptation when you can't be there to help her. That goes for the backyard too—don't leave her unattended outside in the yard if that's a time she might bark at passing dogs.

When you are home and have time to teach your dog not to bark and lunge at dogs passing by, ask for the same responses that you use when outside. As soon as your dog spots an approaching dog, say "Watch" and reinforce right away with something truly wonderful. Remember, the hard part for your dog is to turn her head away from the dog walking by, so reinforce immediately when that furry little head turns toward you. In this case, encourage your dog to turn her head and move away from the window at the same time. You might say "Watch" and then as your dog turns her head, say "Okay!" and run a few steps into the center of the house, encouraging her to come with you. Give the treat or throw the toy well away from the window so she learns to leave the window and move away from it whenever she sees a dog walk by.

Toy-loving dogs are especially easy to teach to switch their attention from what's outside to what's inside. Say "Watch" as soon as they spot another dog out the window, release clearly and toss a toy away from the window. Many dogs, after just a few sessions, will anticipate your watch, turn immediately and run to the toy. Wow! What a dog! This automatic response, just like the Autowatch in your other training, deserves a Jackpot. For ball-crazy dogs, a session of ball play would be just the thing.

Whatever you do to reinforce the right behavior, make it great, and keep working on replacing the problem behavior with one that is acceptable to you and fun for your dog. Whether you use treats or toys, what's important is that your dog learns a new response to an approaching dog, whether she's inside or outside. Your job is to teach her to respond automatically to a passing dog by turning away from it and moving in the other direction, whether it's just looking toward your face, toward a treat, moving toward you to chase you or toward a toy. We've had the best success with a combination of working on this opportunistically and also in organized sessions where friends walk by at pre-arranged times. Be sure that you have your reinforcements easily accessible, so that you are always ready for unexpected passersby.

On the Road

Barking from the car is yet another context that can interfere with having a dog who is polite on leash. Just as you do at home, avoid situations where you're dog is alone in the car and able to bark like a maniac at other dogs. Covered crates can be very handy when you're driving from here to there and can't attend to training while you're driving. When you are able to train (when someone else is driving or if you're parked), wait until you both spot another dog, and either ask your dog to Watch or simply jolly her up with praise and by tossing treats.

It works best to drive to a place where you can predict that you'll see other dogs, and then park so you can concentrate on yours. Pet stores, dog training facilities and veterinarian's offices are always good bets. Park your car at a distance that your dog can handle, and play the Watch game just as you do on the street. Many dogs are worse in cars than on the sidewalk, so don't be surprised if your dog regresses from her behavior in other contexts. If you're working hard on your dog's behavior on walks, you might want to give yourself a break and crate your dog in the car. You don't need to feel the least bit guilty. It's safer for your dog to be in a crate than loose in the car, so it's a good choice no matter how she behaves.

SPECIAL CASES

DOG? WHAT DOG? I DON'T SEE A DOG

Some dogs are so afraid of unfamiliar dogs that they won't even look at one unless the dog is right on top of them. Misty, one of our dogs who is now deceased, was so nervous about unfamiliar dogs that unless the dog was in her face she'd look everywhere but at the dog. At first glance, dogs like Misty look as though they haven't even noticed the other dog, but as you watch more closely, you'll notice that they never look in one particular direction, and that's the direction of the other dog. These dogs have only two responses to the presence of another dog: pretend it's not there if it's far enough away, or explode in a storm of growls and teeth if the dog has gotten too close.

Teaching Watch won't help if your dog is so afraid of other dogs that he won't even look at them. If you have a dog like this, first teach him to look at other dogs on cue. We call this "Where's the Dog?" and it's helped that small percentage of dogs who are so scared of other dogs that they need a little extra help before you can work on Watch and U-Turn. But before you read on, be clear that this technique is only helpful for a small percentage of dog-dog aggressive dogs.

"Where's the Dog?" is not only unnecessary for most dogs, it could get you into trouble with some of them. The last dog to whom you'd want to teach Where's the Dog? is a "lock and load" dog, who goes out of his way to give long, hard stares to other dogs. You'll also want to avoid using it with dogs who are doing what ethologists call a "look away." These dogs will look toward another dog if it isn't too close, but will turn their heads during social encounters as a way to defuse social tension. (Similar in some ways to a Watch, in that it avoids direct eye contact.) Don't take this valuable part of your dog's social repertoire away. There is only one type of dog who profits from Where's the Dog?: a dog who consistently avoids looking at any unfamiliar dog, no matter how far away, but who explodes in an attack if the dog gets too close.

Teaching "Where's the Dog?"

Start as you would with any new exercise, teaching Where's the Dog? in a quiet place with few distractions. Since you can't teach Where's the Dog? without another dog around, you need to be thoughtful about where to have your first sessions. You need a place in which the other dog is managed with a fence or leash so that you can control the distance between the dogs. You must be confident that an unfamiliar dog won't get too close and set your dog off. Pick a place where the logistics allow you to keep your dog from becoming aroused. You can manage your dog's arousal by either keeping him far away from an unfamiliar dog, or by using a dog that he knows well and reacts to politely. Needless to say, a familiar dog who gets only happy reactions from your dog can be a lot closer than unfamiliar ones.

Ideally, you'll have a set of dear friends who love dogs as much as you do and will agree to walk their calm, non-reactive dog down the sidewalk at pre-arranged times several times a week. Yeah, well, we said that was ideal. If you don't have a pool of people with nothing else to do but help you out, choose a place where you know that other dogs will be on leash (entering dog training class, entering a vet clinic, etc.), and position yourself a good, long distance away. You want the other dog to be close enough that your dog will notice it, but far enough away that your dog is calm and still able to pay attention to you. If you can do this with a friend all the better; it's always nice to have someone to help.

When the other dog comes into view, say "Where's the Dog?" in a clear, happy voice. If by some miracle your dog does look at the other dog, immediately mark that behavior by saying "Good," or with a click if your dog is clicker savvy. Then give your dog a great treat in the very next second. Timing is always critical in training, but this is one cue that requires especially good timing, because it can be difficult for your dog to figure out what he's getting rewarded for. Is the treat for looking to the left, looking at the human with the dog, looking at something that's moving? It's not that easy to be sure that your dog understands what he's being reinforced for, so help him out by being precise. This is a great application for the attention-getting sound and precision of a clicker.

He Won't Look at Another Dog and I Can't Get Him to Read This Booklet

If your dog won't look at the other dog (that is, after all, the problem you're working on!) don't try to force him. Avoid pointing and coaxing, not to mention begging and pleading, because that just keeps the attention on you. It's much more effective to have the person with the other dog move around in a circle, or take a few steps to the side. Most dogs are attracted to motion, even at the edge of their peripheral vision, so arrange for the other dog to move and say "Where's the Dog?" as he does. The other person can also make a noise such as throat clearing, clapping, or smooching, but drop this out as soon as you can. You want your dog to look at other dogs, not other humans. You might need to shape resistant dogs by reinforcing a look in the right direction, even if it's not directly at the other dog.

When Opportunity Knocks

If your dog just happens to look at another dog, seize this golden opportunity and make the most of it. Say "Good" as he does, and then Jackpot him so that he's as thrilled as you are about the whole process. If you've started with dogs far enough away, and if you're using a reinforcement that your dog just adores, your dog will most likely be looking at other dogs within three to five sessions. Once he reliably starts offering the behavior, you can start working on Watch. Lucky for us, Where's the Dog? often begins to evolve all by itself into a Watch. Dogs who are taught Where's the Dog? quickly learn to look at their owners for their treat right after they've looked at another dog. Sounds like a Watch to us, so don't be discouraged if your dog needs to learn Where's the Dog? before you work on Watch. Your dog is simply telling you how truly anxious he is about other dogs, and he'll be ever so grateful that you are trying to help him out.

ABANDONMENT TRAINING

This is a technique originally described by John Fisher, in which an owner turns and deserts his dog if the dog behaves aggressively. In Fisher's version, the owner immediately leaves the dog's sight at any sign of impolite behavior, usually disappearing through a well-placed door. Several top trainers, including Trish King of the Marin Humane Society and Pia Silvani of St. Hubert's Animal Welfare Center, have made their own adaptations to this method, and when done with the right dog, the results can be dramatic.

In all cases, Abandonment training works best on dogs who are a bit insecure and a bit clingy with their owners. It also works best on dogs who react problematically to any and all dogs, (rather than particular types of dogs) and on dogs who don't have a long history of bad behavior when on leash. It might also be a good technique for dogs who are worse if they are close to their owners. Some of these dogs may be possessive of their owners and aggress toward other dogs who get too close. Owners often report that these dogs are "protecting them," when in reality, the dog is protecting his access to his owner. "She's my bone and I'm NOT sharing" is a good translation. If what your dog wants is access to you, it can be powerful to take "you" away at any sign of rude behavior.

In one version of Abandonment training, the owner turns and runs like heck the other way at the slightest sign of aggressive behavior from his dog. Unlike U-Turns, the owner makes no attempt to encourage the dog to turn, rather she uses a verbal cue like "Bye" or "Oops," throws the six-foot leash onto the dog's back as a tactile cue (not a correction), and dashes off, leaving her dog "abandoned" in the dust. This dramatic method is safe because someone else is holding a 20-foot line that is also attached to the dog, and the line acts as a safety net that keeps the dog out of trouble. The line should not restrict the dog in any way, except from charging at the other dogs and generally making an idiot of himself. One advantage of this method is that the owner can turn and dash away from the dog without having to worry about what her dog will do, and concentrate on running away.

As usual, you'll want to set up the initial training sessions so that all goes according to plan. Have a friend or relative with a calm, leashed dog walking toward you and your dog. You're ready with both a six-foot leash and a 20-foot line on your dog, with a trained friend or trainer holding the long line. At the very first indication that your dog is becoming aroused, whether it's a snarl, a stiffening, or a growl, quickly say "Bye," throw your leash so that it hits your dog's back, then turn and run away. The person holding the long line runs along with the dog, insuring that it doesn't inadvertently stop him just as he turns to run to you. When your dog catches up to you, Jackpot him effusively as if he had just won Westminster.

With all dogs, we suspect that running after an owner acts as a wonderful reinforcement. Most dogs adore running with their humans, and not many get to do so. We think it's highly under-rated as a powerful reinforcement. Even if Abandonment training isn't for your dog, you might want to add a quick run as reinforcement for a good U-Turn. In some ways, U-Turns and this version of Abandonment are similar: in both, the owner rapidly turns away from an approaching dog and the dog learns it's fun to follow. U-Turns suggest that you teach the action as a behavior you've shaped and reinforced through an increasingly difficult set of distractions. Abandonment doesn't so much teach what "right" is, rather it creates a consequence for the "wrong" behavior. With dogs who are clingy and afraid of losing their owners, that consequence can be powerful indeed.

The other useful version of Abandonment training starts with your dog safely tethered on a tie-out as well as on a leash held by the owner's. Another dog is brought into view, and if the feisty fido shows the slightest sign of reactivity, the owner abruptly drops the leash and strides out of the room. The reactive dog is left abandoned to cope for himself. The approaching dog, safely managed on leash of course, stands quietly. When the dog-in-training stops being inappropriate, the owner returns. This method is most effective on dogs who are especially clingy, and are simply stunned when their owners disappear. We like to combine this with lots of positive reinforcement, so that the dog learns an appropriate behavior as well as inhibiting an inappropriate one.

If Abandonment training will help your dog, you'll know it after just three or four attempts. If it doesn't help a great deal after just a few tries, then it's probably not the right method for you. We don't mean that your dog should be magically cured, but you should see some impressive improvement relatively early on. If you don't, you might have a dog who just gets more aroused with movement, and will profit more from the quiet focus of a steady Watch cue.

CONCLUSION

Successful work with a feisty fido requires that you become a bit of a boy scout—always prepared. With prevention, an emergency plan, a solid Watch and mastery of the U-Turn, you and your dog can handle just about anything. Granted, that can be a lot of work. But surely it's worth it when your neighbors refer to you as the owner of "that" dog and mean the sweet, wonderful dog who's the neighborhood role model. That's a great reward in itself. We wish we could include even more reinforcement for you for being such a committed, responsible dog owner. Chocolate maybe? Surely you deserve your own Jackpot. But the chocolate kept melting in the printing press, so we'll simply extend a sincere thank you for caring so much about your dog's manners. Good luck, keep the faith and go tell your dog that life is going to get a whole lot better, really soon.

SUGGESTED BOOKS AND VIDEOS

Here are some books and videos that might be helpful for anyone with a feisty fido. This list is not extensive, but is a good start for anyone who would like some more resources.

Aloff, Brenda. 2002
Aggression in Dogs: Practical Management, Prevention, & Behavior Modification.

Booth, Sheila. 1998
Purely Positive Training: Companion to Competition.

Campbell, William. 1999
Behavior Problems in Dogs.

Dunbar, Ian. 1998
Video: Dog Aggression: Biting and Fighting

Hetts, Suzanne and Estep, Daniel. 2002
Video: Canine Behavior Program: Body Postures and Evaluating Behavioral Health

Landsberg, G., Hunthausen, W. and Ackerman, L. 1997
Handbook of behavior problems of the dog and cat.

London, Karen B. and McConnell, Patricia B. 2001
Feeling Outnumbered? How to Manage and Enjoy Your Multi-Dog Household.

McAuliffe, Claudeen. 2001
Lucy Won't Sit

McConnell, Patricia B. 1998
The Cautious Canine: How to Help Dogs Conquer Their Fears

Miller, Pat.
The Power of Positive Dog Training

Reid, Pamela J. 1996
*Excel-erated Learning: Explaining in Plain English How Dogs
Learn and How Best to Teach Them*

Ryan, Terry. 1998
The Toolbox for Remodeling Your Problem Dog

Sternberg, Sue. 2000
Dog to Dog Aggression Video